Cheetahs

by Claire Archer

ABDO
BIG CATS
Kids

Visit us at www.abdopublishing.com

Published by Abdo Kids, a division of ABDO, P.O. Box 398166, Minneapolis, Minnesota 55439.

Copyright © 2015 by Abdo Consulting Group, Inc. International copyrights reserved in all countries.
No part of this book may be reproduced in any form without written permission from the publisher.

Printed in the United States of America, North Mankato, Minnesota.

032014

092014

 PRINTED ON RECYCLED PAPER

Photo Credits: Shutterstock, Thinkstock

Production Contributors: Teddy Borth, Jennie Forsberg, Grace Hansen

Design Contributors: Dorothy Toth, Renée LaViolette, Laura Rask

Library of Congress Control Number: 2013952087

Cataloging-in-Publication Data

Archer, Claire.

Cheetahs / Claire Archer.

  p. cm. -- (Big cats)

ISBN 978-1-62970-001-4 (lib. bdg.)

Includes bibliographical references and index.

1. Cheetahs--Juvenile literature.   I. Title.

599.75--dc23

                    2013952087

Table of Contents

Cheetahs

Cheetahs live in Africa and Asia. You can find them in the grassy **plains** and open **savannas**.

4

Cheetahs are big cats. Lions

and tigers are big cats too.

7

Cheetahs have light brown fur with black spots. They have stripes on their tails.

Cheetahs have tear-shaped **markings** around their eyes. It looks like they have tears running down their faces.

Cheetahs do not roar like other big cats. Cheetahs purr, hiss, and growl.

Fast Cats

Cheetahs are the fastest animals on land. They can run up to 70 mph (113 kph)!

15

Hunting

Cheetahs hunt during the day.
Most other big cats hunt
mainly at night.

16

17

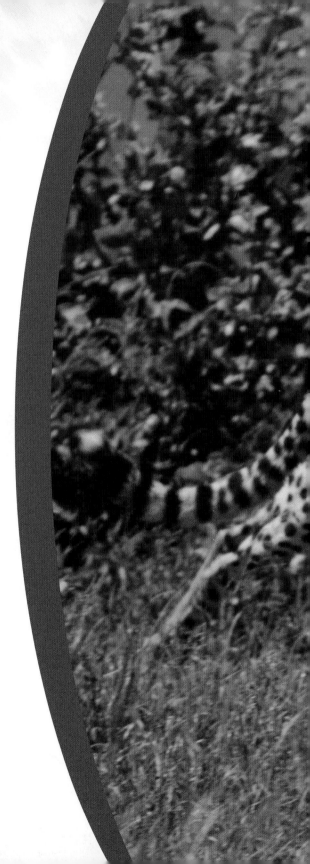

Food

Cheetahs are meat eaters.

They eat animals like gazelle, antelope, and birds.

18

19

Baby Cheetahs

Female cheetahs have two to five babies at a time. Baby cheetahs are called **cubs**.

More Facts

- Cheetahs use their tails to steer themselves while running.

- Cheetahs cannot climb trees.

- After the cheetah catches its **prey**, it has to wait about 30 minutes to eat. It needs to catch its breath!

- Cheetah **cubs** have a lot of **predators**. Their mothers put them in new hiding places every few days. Mothers must leave their cubs alone when they hunt.

Glossary

cub – a young animal.

marking – a mark or pattern of marks on an animal's fur, feathers, or skin.

plain – an area of dry, grassy land.

predator - an animal that hunts others.

prey - an animal hunted or killed by a predator for food.

savanna – a grassland with few or no trees.

Index

abdokids.com

Use this code to log on to abdokids.com and access crafts, games, videos and more!

Abdo Kids Code:
BCK0014